The Ghost in the Washing Machine

Compiled by John Foster

Illustrated by Leo Broadley, Agnese Baruzzi,
Lee Cosgrove, Sara Ogilvie, Galia Bernstein, Yannick Robert,
Laura Ellen Anderson, Sole Otero, Emi Ordás
and Olga Demidova

OXFORD
UNIVERSITY PRESS

Contents

There was a Young Man Called Pete

There was a young man called Pete
Who stood on his head in the street.
He said, 'It is clear,
If I remain here,
I shall have to shake hands with my feet.'

Anon

Uncle's Robot

My uncle built a robot.
He gave it to his nieces.
It walked into a wall,
went CLUNK! and fell to pieces.

Charles Thomson

What is written on a robot's tombstone?

Rust in Peace.

How does a robot know when it's attractive?

When bits of metal stick to it.

When the Robot went to the Doctor

The robot was not feeling well.
He went to the doctor, who said,
'You need some minor repairs.
There's a rusty bolt loose in your head.'

The doctor picked up a spanner.
'This only takes a minute or two.'
He poured some oil round the nut
And carefully began to unscrew.

He removed the loose rusty bolt
And screwed a new one in place.
'That'll do the trick,' he said with a smile.
But the robot just gave a grimace.

He lifted himself off the workbench,
Gave a grunt and then a roar,
And, knocking the doctor unconscious,
He smashed through the surgery door.

The robot went storming down the street,
Scowling at passers-by,
While the doctor came round in the surgery
With a headache and a black eye.

Chris Whitby

Superhero's Diary

MONDAY

Turned back alien invasion fleet attacking planet Mars.

TUESDAY

Tried out my latest powered boots by going round the stars.

WEDNESDAY

Held up collapsing building after severe earthquake.

THURSDAY

Retrieved a nuclear missile fired by mistake.

FRIDAY

Kept afloat a sinking ship till safely on the shore.

SATURDAY

Planned with other heroes to stop war for ever more.

Hit my thumb with hammer while repairing garden shed.
Made me feel all faint and funny; spent the afternoon in bed.

Alan Priestley

If Batman is so cool,
why does he wear his
underpants OUTSIDE
his trousers?

SuperMum

I'm a superheroine.
By day I'm just a mum.
But at night when there is trouble
You can call me and I'll come.

I've pulled survivors from the wreckage
Of a burning plane.
I've rescued a man who was trapped
In a flooded drain.

I've saved a ship from sinking
By towing it ashore.
I've freed a hostage who was held
Behind an iron door.

SHIP SAVED BY
MYSTERY
SUPERHERO

I've defused ticking time bombs
By cutting through the wires.
I've dragged unconscious people
Out of blazing fires.

I'm known as SuperMum
And you will often see
On the front page of a newspaper
A picture of me.

My children laugh and say,
'Doesn't she look like you!'
Wouldn't they have a surprise
If only they knew!

Pam Johnson

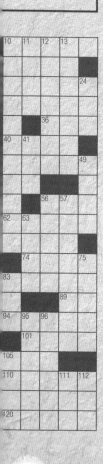

Lonely Hearts

Superheroine –
  nine feet high (with own cape)
  wishes to meet
Superhero –
for outings to:

- 💜 burning buildings
- 💜 haunted castles
- 💜 snake pits
- 💜 and sinking ships.

Also foreign travel – Mars, Mercury, Jupiter, etc.

MUST like:

- 💜 clubs (karate)
- 💜 clothes (combat)
- 💜 bombs (unexploded)
- 💜 and car-driving – preferably off cliffs.

Also: pets – piranhas, sharks, poisonous reptiles.
Please include photo (no masks).

Peter Dixon

Soulmate Wanted

Lonely witch,
haggard and dishevelled, would
like to meet spell-qualified wizard
interested in scare-sharing
and toad-making.

Pam Johnson

An angry witch burst into the baker's shop and said, 'I sent my black cat to buy a kilo of biscuits this morning, but when I weighed them there was only half a kilo. I suggest you check your scales.' The baker looked at her calmly and replied, 'Madam, I suggest you weigh your cat.'

FOR SALE – One Broomstick

One broomstick.
Over 1,000 flights.
Fully serviced by
Groans & Frights.

One previous owner,
Now retired.
Twelve-stroke engine,
Diesel fired.

Padded ejector seat.
Retractable landing gear.
Insured and taxed
Until leap year.

All offers considered.
Contact: A. Sprite
At Hecate's Cavern,
After midnight.

Pam Johnson

The Artist

I painted a brilliant picture
The greatest ever seen.
It hung in the National Gallery
And was purchased by the Queen.
This most wonderful of paintings
Is called 'Polar Bears in the Snow'
And in case you don't believe me
I've included it below.

Gareth Owen

Polar Bears in the Snow

Why is it difficult to keep a secret at the North Pole?

Because your teeth keep chattering.

What sort of athlete would be warmest at the North Pole?

A long jumper.

At Windsor Castle

At Windsor Castle
The Queen's been seen
Jumping up and down
On a trampoline.

Derek Stuart

Ouch!

The young ghost had a bad headache.
The reason was plain, you see.
He tried to come in through the keyhole,
But someone had left in the key.

Ian Ashendon

Vanished

'I'm looking for books on mysterious disappearances,'
Said the customer. 'I've looked everywhere.'
'I'm sorry,' said the librarian.
'They used to be over there.'

Evie Lewis

What is even more invisible than the invisible man?

The invisible man's shadow.

Why did the invisible man look in the mirror?

He wanted to make sure he wasn't there.

The Ghost in the Washing Machine

A ghost is stuck in our washing machine,
And I say serves him right.
He got mixed up with the sheet, you see,
And now he's whiter than white.

His eyes are staring, he's really glaring,
He's not enjoying the ride.
I'll set him free at half past three,
As soon as he's tumble-dried.

Kaye Umansky

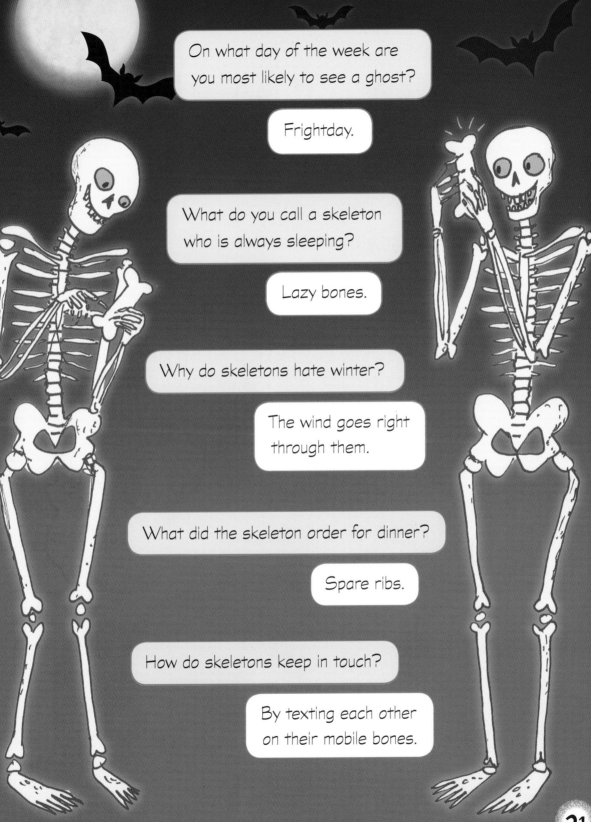

On what day of the week are you most likely to see a ghost?

Frightday.

What do you call a skeleton who is always sleeping?

Lazy bones.

Why do skeletons hate winter?

The wind goes right through them.

What did the skeleton order for dinner?

Spare ribs.

How do skeletons keep in touch?

By texting each other on their mobile bones.

Have You Ever?

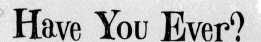

Have you ever seen a fox learning how to box?
Have you ever played leapfrog with a dog?
Have you skated on the ice with a family of mice?
Have you ever had a chat with a rat?

Have you sat on a bus beside a hippopotamus?
Have you rowed across a lake with a snake?
Have you sat on a pillar playing chess with a gorilla?
Have you ridden in a boat with a goat?

Have you played a game of bingo with a flamingo?
Have you swum in the dark with a shark?
Have you paddled a canoe beside a kangaroo?
Have you ever seen an elephant fly?

You haven't? Well, neither have I!

Derek Stuart

A man took his elephant to the cinema. The manager expected it to go on the rampage, but it didn't. Afterwards he said to the man, 'I'm surprised your elephant sat quietly and seemed to enjoy the film.'

'Yes,' said the man. 'I'm surprised too. He didn't like the book.'

Batty Books

Tall Stories by G. Raffe

From Trunk to Tail *by Ellie Phant*

The Art of Butting by Billy Goat

Great Snakes by Anna Conda

Snaphappy by Allie Gator

Insect Bites by Amos Quito

An Ass's Tale by Don Key

It's a Dog's Life *by Jack Russell*

Glow-Worm

The young glow-worm said, in a fright,
'I cannot produce any light.
Is there any way of knowing
Why I have stopped glowing?
Am I going to be all right?'

His mother said,
'I know what the matter is.
What you need is a change of batteries.'

John Foster

Why was the glow-worm unhappy?

Because her children weren't very bright.

One goldfish swimming in a goldfish bowl
said to another goldfish, 'Why do you keep
following me around?'

A Daring Young Girl Called Rita

A daring young girl called Rita,
One day had a race with a cheetah.
But she was defeated,
Since the cheetah cheated.
'Cause to beat her the cheetah ate Rita.

John Foster

Hare and the Tortoise

When the hare raced the tortoise
And the tortoise won
The hare was very dejected.
The tortoise was driving a Porsche 911
So the outcome was not unexpected.

Roger Stevens

A Jaguar from Zanzibar

A jaguar from Zanzibar
Became a famous movie star,
Winning an Oscar for the part
He played in *Big Cat Stole My Heart*.
So now he lies by the pool each day
Outside his mansion in LA.

Derek Stuart

Ostrich

One morning
an ostrich
buried his head
in the sand
and fell asleep.
On waking,
he couldn't remember
where he buried it.

Roger McGough

Blame

ABC
$a^2 + b^2 = c^2$

Graham, look at Maureen's leg,
She says you tried to tattoo it!
I did, Miss, yes – with my biro,
But Jonathan told me to do it.

Graham, look at Peter's sock,
It's got a burn-hole through it!
It was just an experiment, Miss, with the lens.
Jonathan told me to do it.

Alice's bag is stuck to the floor.
Look, Graham, did you glue it?
Yes, but I never thought it would work,
And Jonathan told me to do it.

Jonathan, what's all this I hear
About you and Graham Prewitt?
Well, Miss, it's really more his fault:
He *tells* me to tell him to do it.

Allan Ahlberg

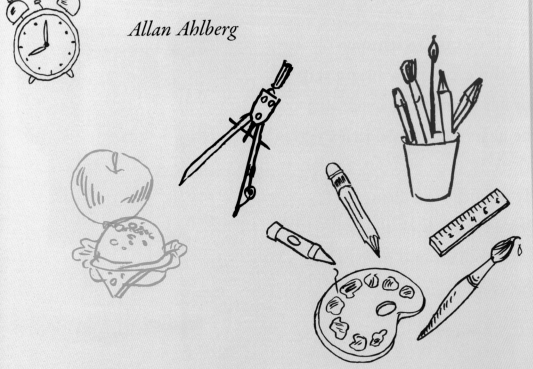

My Teacher is an Alien

My teacher is an alien.
She knows everything we do.
She has eyes in the back of her head,
Which are always watching you.

If you are planning to write a note
Or to make a paper dart,
Her antennae will tell her at once
Before you even start.

And if you try to whisper
Her three ears glow bright red,
For her hearing's so acute,
She hears every word that's said.

My teacher is an alien.
Of that there is no doubt.
If you fool around in *her* class,
She's sure to find you out.

Ian Ashendon

When the Alien Landed in our Street

When the alien landed in our street,
We all went out to greet her.
But she ignored all of us
And spoke to a parking meter.

When the parking meter didn't reply,
She thought, *What a funny race.*
So she climbed into her spacecraft
And flew back into space.

Simon Sharples

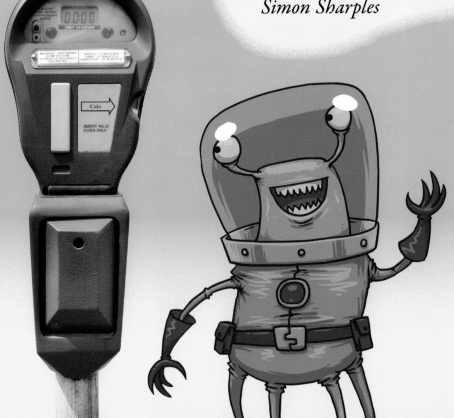

About John Foster

I grew up in Carlisle and dreamed of
playing football for Carlisle United,
but they showed no interest in signing me. After
working as a firefighter in Canada, I became a teacher.
That's when I started to write poems and edit poetry
books. I've written about 1,500 poems and compiled over
100 anthologies. But none of them have been as much fun
as compiling the Chucklers anthologies.

I've chuckled at the jaguar who has become a movie star
and the tortoise driving a Porsche, giggled at the witch
who has placed a lonely hearts advert for a soulmate,
laughed at the ghost who's trapped in a washing machine,
and chortled at a queen bouncing up and down on
a trampoline.